OHIO RAILROADS

OHIO RAILROADS

C. S. GISCOMBE

OMNIDAWN PUBLISHING
RICHMOND, CALIFORNIA
2014

Cover image: Railroad Crossing at Stony Hollow Road, Dayton, Ohio
Courtesy of the Ohio Rail Development Commission and
the Public Utilities Commission of Ohio

Interior images:

Map of the Dayton Union Railway, 1952 is from the
Annual Summary Report of the New York Central Raiload System, 1953

Map of the Pennsylvania Railroad, c. 1950 is from the archives of the Pennsylvania Railroad

Map of Dayton Railroads, 1875 and
Map of Western Region of New France, or Canada, 1755
(also know as Jacques Nicolas Bellin's 1755 map,
Partie Occidentale de la Nouvelle France ou du Canada)
are courtesy of the Library of Congress

Cover and Interior Design by Cassandra Smith

Typefaces: Adobe Caslon Pro, Adobe Jensen Pro, and Waters Titling Pro.

Offset printed in the United States
by Edwards Brothers Malloy, Ann Arbor, Michigan
On 55# Enviro Natural 100% Recycled 100% PCW
Acid Free Archival Quality FSC Certified Paper
with Rainbow FSC Certified Colored End Papers

Published by Omnidawn Publishing, Richmond, California
www.omnidawn.com   (510) 237-5472   (800) 792-4957
10 9 8 7 6 5 4 3 2 1
ISBN: 978-1-890650-74-2

HAVING DREAMT YEARS PREVIOUSLY of seeing my mother's death falling, indistinguishable from rain, on a railroad bridge at the eastern end of Dayton's downtown business district, I went out purposely on the day after she did die—the 3rd of August 2008, her death having occurred on the 2nd—to see the bridge itself on East Third Street. It was standing as I recalled it in the dream but I'd seen and passed under the bridge many times in my own early life in Dayton—it was the furthest edge of downtown, the obvious boundary, or monument of boundary, between downtown and the tough white neighborhoods beyond downtown, east of it. She—my mother—had come to Dayton in 1949 with her new husband, when she was twenty-five, from St. Louis, where she had lived with her parents, where she'd taught in the public schools. She had a Master's degree in Education from the University of Michigan; in Ann Arbor she had lived in a residence hall and some of the white women there, her fellow graduate students, asked her to help them in their petition to force the handful of black students to eat together consistently, to take each meal at the same cafeteria table, not realizing that she was black.

In Dayton, from the 1940s until the mid-1970s, black people lived west of the Great Miami River, the water that forms the western limit of downtown; in 2008, the term of description, the West Side, still meant black Dayton, though in fact black people in 2008 lived in all parts of Dayton except Oakwood. Third Street is the primary east-west street in Dayton: it traverses both the West Side and East Dayton and it provides the division, across the city, for the north-south running streets. That is, streets that cross Third Street are designated "North" north of the intersection and "South" to the south of their meeting with Third Street. Third Street crosses the river on a gently arched bridge and at the bridge's western end are the blocks that form the principal business district of the West Side; at the eastern foot of the bridge lie the beginnings of downtown Dayton—the Safety Building (the multi-storey city police headquarters), the Y.W.C.A., the campus of Sinclair Community College. But downtown, even across the river, Third Street is West Third Street until its intersection, at the old Montgomery County Courthouse, with Main Street; it's East Third Street after that. East Third Street at the railroad bridge, a mile and a half east of the bridge over the Great Miami, is still wide.

When I went out to look at the railroad bridge on the day following my mother's death, East Third Street was a river of traffic and lanes of cars, trucks, and trolley buses flowed underneath and between the cement supports; the street was busy even though it was a Sunday. I'd taken pains, at the time I had dreamt of the bridge, to write down details of what I had seen and later I described the dream in a poem, noting that though the bridge I saw in the dream was over Third Street, the actual bridge snakes across all of downtown Dayton and has "high cement sides"; that is, the tracks that cross downtown are elevated, they cross downtown above street level and the elevation is itself skirted by a cement wall, twenty-five feet or so high, that runs from Wilkinson Street, in the west, to East Third Street. The downtown streets cross the tracks through gaps—underpasses—in this wall; it's possible to consider each of these crossings to be a bridge (over this street, over that street) but it's necessary as well to see the whole structure—the elevation across which the tracks are laid and the cement walls beneath that, at either side of it—as a single bridge across the whole of downtown. The span at East Third Street is only the final moment in that single bridge.

2.

In 2008 the Dayton railroads continued to operate along right-of-ways that had been planned and graded and built into Dayton or through Dayton in the latter half of the 19th century. The railroads come in from Cincinnati to the southwest, from Toledo to the north, and from Columbus—the state capital—to the northeast. The history of railroads is a history of mergers and in 2008 only two companies served the city, the Norfolk Southern and the Chessie System (or CSX); a diminishing web of industrial tracks supplied and continues to supply the manufacturers. In the 1950s and 1960s—my childhood and teenage years in Dayton—the Norfolk Southern was the New York Central and CSX was the Baltimore and Ohio. The Pennsylvania Railroad connected Dayton to St. Louis—one of the many towns called "Gateway to the West"—and to New York and now those tracks are gone, the railroad grade is now a paved recreational trail in many places both east and west of Dayton. The last time I came to Dayton by rail I arrived from New York, in 1975 or 1976. The CSX tracks and the Norfolk Southern tracks follow the valley of the Great Miami River between Dayton and Cincinnati; they are often visible from one another, not a unique situation when railroads compete. The two lines come together in Dayton at the grade crossing at Washington Street and a quarter mile later are joined by what was the Pennsylvania's St. Louis line (that now, operated by CSX, extends only as far as International Molasses on Wolf Creek Pike, at the furthest western edge of Dayton). From this perspective, facing east from the Washington Street railroad crossing on the near West Side, the tracks—the two lines from Cincinnati and the one line from the confectionary—all cross the Great Miami on a single truss bridge of three spans and enter downtown together as what was known, in the last century, as the Dayton Union Railway; an embankment carries the tracks until the elevated structure begins at Wilkinson Street, where the train station was.

[MAP OF DAYTON UNION RAILWAY, 1952]

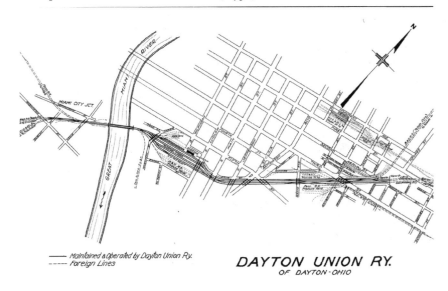

—— Maintained & Operated by Dayton Union Ry.
----- Foreign Lines

DAYTON UNION RY.
OF DAYTON - OHIO

At the eastern end of downtown the railroad tracks divide again into three lines. The CSX and the Norfolk Southern cross East Third Street on the railroad bridge I had dreamt about and then the CSX, turning north, crosses the Miami River for the second time within the city, on a plate-girder bridge, but follows the river's valley up through Tipp City, Troy, Piqua, etc.; Tipp City was originally named Tippecanoe City to honor William Henry Harrison's 1811 victory over Tecumseh's Confederation at the Battle of Tippecanoe, in present-day Indiana. Harrison was eventually elected president of the United States but died after a month in office. Tippecanoe City's name was changed in the 1930s to avoid confusion with the other Tippecanoe in Harrison County—named also for William Henry Harrison—in eastern Ohio; George Armstrong Custer was from Harrison County, from New Rumley—the foundations of his birthplace remain and the site is marked with a statue. New Rumley has no railroad; an old map of the Cleveland, Lorain, and Wheeling Railroad—now part of CSX—shows a station at Tippecanoe, which sat at the edge of a shaded portion of the map labeled "Coal Territory," but those tracks are gone. Tippecanoe is far from Dayton. From Dayton, the Norfolk Southern goes northeast along the Mad River, skirting the edge of the Wright-Patterson Air Force base, heading for Springfield and, beyond that, Columbus. Many people believe that Wright-Patterson houses alien bodies from the Roswell, New Mexico flying saucer crash of 1947; Oliver "Pappy" Henderson claimed, to his wife and daughter and to a number of others as well,

to have flown the dead aliens and debris from the spacecraft in a
C-54 transport plane from Roswell to "Wright Field" in Dayton.
He described the bodies to his wife as "small with large heads for
their size" and, to his daughter, as "humanoid-looking, but different
from us." He described the wreckage to John Kromschroeder as
"spacecraft garbage"; he said, "The passengers suffered their death."
Henderson was called "Pappy" because he was older than the other
pilots in his squadron." Tecumseh had been born on the Mad River,
at Old Piqua, in 1768.

The former Pennsylvania track diverges from the Norfolk
Southern and CXS routes before the East Third Street bridge.
It swings off due east and parallels Third Street (the other tracks
span Third Street at a forty-five degree angle); the track—wavy in
2008, infrequently used—proceeds at street level and is punctuated
by grade crossings as it crosses East Dayton. This had been, until
1976, one of the Pennsylvania Railroad's main lines, the Panhandle
Route: from Dayton it had continued ten miles to Xenia, Ohio
before tilting north to go through Columbus and then on east
across West Virginia and into Pittsburgh before going over the
Allegheny Mountains and eventually reaching New York. It was
called the Panhandle Route because it crossed the narrow West
Virginia panhandle; it's a thick line on the railroad maps (as
opposed to the thin lines, on the same maps, which indicate lighter
traffic) of Ohio, Indiana, and Illinois.

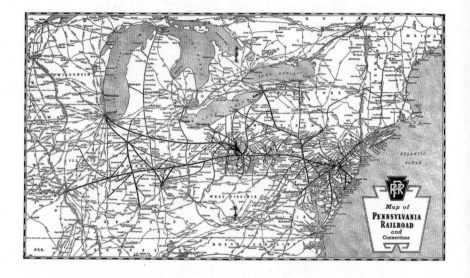

The Pennsylvania's signature passenger train between New York and St. Louis, the Spirit of St. Louis (for Charles Lindbergh's airplane), had used the Panhandle Route. In present-day Dayton the route does not extend beyond Linden Avenue—it's only a stub to some industries; east of town, however, the bridges that carried the tracks over the north-south roads between Dayton and Xenia, the seats of government for Montgomery and Greene Counties, are still in place, visible from the Route 35 expressway. The Pennsylvania, in 1916, began using the slogan, "Standard Railroad of the World"; it merged with the

New York Central in 1968 to form the Penn Central, which became part of Conrail, the government-run Consolidated Rail Corporation, in 1976. Xenia had been a rail system crossroads though no tracks remain now; the Pennsylvania's line between Cincinnati and Columbus had had a station at Xenia and, south of Xenia, had followed the curves of the Little Miami River as it—the river—came past Fort Ancient. The "Pennsylvania Railroad and Connections" map indicates that the railroad exists or existed as a straight line south of Xenia but in fact the river's twists had governed the path of construction. Work on the Little Miami Railroad—the name under which the line was originally incorporated—began in 1837 and by 1845 train service was in place between Cincinnati and Xenia. In 1869, the Little Miami leased all its property to a consortium, which included the Pennsylvania Railroad, "for 99 years, renewable forever"; the Pennsylvania renewed the lease in 1968 but by 1972, during the Penn Central era, had begun to remove the tracks.

Xenia always had a black population; the WPA's Ohio Guide had used weighted language in the "Washington Court House to Indiana Line" tour to suggest that there was abundant racism behind the city's pleasant appearance. Two black colleges—Central State and Wilberforce University—are located in Wilberforce, Ohio, a census designated place (or CDP) lying four miles northeast of Xenia; "census designated place" is the new name (as of 1950) for "unincorporated place." The latter black school, Wilberforce University, was founded in 1856, "prior to the end of slavery." The white abolitionist William Wilberforce, for whom the school was named, had been born in

England (in Hull, in Yorkshire) in 1759 and died in 1833. The Pennsylvania tracks north to Yellow Springs—also part of the railroad's Little Miami Branch—were laid down Detroit Street in Xenia; that is, they were embedded in Detroit Street's pavement. By the early 1960s service north of the city—Xenia—was sporadic and people visiting from elsewhere, unfamiliar with the practice or idea of "street-running," were often shocked to see a train, even a slow-moving one, in the street; the tracks between Xenia and Yellow Springs had been gone for more than thirty years but were still indicated in 2008 on Google Maps. Yellow Springs, the site of Antioch College, is nine miles north of Xenia and the railroad's right of way between the two places has been made into a bicycle trail. Yellow Springs is known as "the most miscegenated place in America" but in Dayton, according to stories, it was common, as early as the 1940s, to see Negroes walking downtown with their white girlfriends. In 2008 my father remembered Xenia in the 1950s as "a country town." Black people there had cafes in the front or back rooms of their houses, he said; it was common knowledge which houses offered meals but the cafes were never advertised. When Amtrak took over the United States' passenger train service the Spirit of St. Louis was renamed National Limited and the run was extended to Kansas City. At that time the station stop at Xenia was eliminated. Sometimes, however, the east- and west-bound National Limited trains would meet at Xenia; this would necessitate one train backing down or heading down the Little Miami Branch south and then emerging after the other train had cleared, the Dayton Line—as it was called locally—being single track.

In Dayton, the Pennsylvania Railroad maintained two manned crossing towers, both of which were in black Dayton. Germantown Street, the Pennsylvania's first crossing on the West Side, had no tower but it did have a guard through the early 1960s—a light-skinned older man would step into the street, as a train approached, with a STOP sign on a pole. Germantown Street begins when West Fifth Street splits after crossing the river and proceeds, carrying Ohio Route 4, in a straight line southwest to the city limit where it curves to assume a slightly more southerly trajectory and becomes Germantown Pike. In Dayton it passes Wogoman School, the Dayton Metropolitan Housing Authority's DeSoto Bass Courts, the Bowman Funeral Chapel, some small markets and restaurants, and then climbs sharply to meet Mount Clair Avenue and skirt the Veterans Administration campus. The Channel 7/ WHIO tower is at the very top of the climb; it occupies the same high ground as the Veterans Administration. Below the television station's tower is the Workhouse, the Dayton Correctional Institute. According to stories, the Soap Box Derby had used Germantown Hill, as Germantown Street between Mount Clair Avenue and McArthur Avenue is called, until the ignominy of having a national event on Dayton's West Side got the better of the Derby's organizers. The Pennsylvania Railroad's Germantown Street crossing was protected by automatic flashing lights in addition to the guard but its crossings further down the line on West Fifth Street and on heavily traveled West Third Street had no flashing lights to warn motorists of an approaching train; instead, at each of those latter two crossings, a railroad man in a trackside tower would lower large wooden gates from their vertical position at the curb to a horizontal one across all the lanes of Fifth Street and Third Street when a train came. In the 1960s there were many trains each day, both freight and passenger. The gates were striped, black and white. In the midst of West Side business on Third Street the trains looked slightly out of scale; "Tuscan Red" was the Pennsylvania's passenger color—it was a dusky flat red on the sides of the "bulldog nose" locomotives and the coaches. The railroad crossing was at the bottom of the Third Street hill, at river level. Approaching on Third Street from the west one would come to the intersection with Summit Street and suddenly have a view of both the crossing and, beside it, the large Kroger chain store which, with its excavated hillside parking lot, was an anchor of the West Side commercial district; the intersection was the top of the Third Street hill (as Summit Street's name would suggest) and the downtown skyline, beyond the river, was also visible from there. Trains seemed to dwarf the Kroger store as they passed next to it. The railroad, after crossing the river, curved through the West Side and followed Wolf Creek northwest to and beyond the city line, coming to Trotwood and then Brookville before turning west to Richmond, Indianapolis, Effingham, and St. Louis.

3.

Paul Laurence Dunbar's house was on North Summit Street, now renamed North Paul Laurence Dunbar Street. The street is unusually wide for a residential area and, in 2008, still had a brick surface beyond its intersection with West Third Street; Paul Laurence Dunbar Street is slightly west of the limits of the Wright-Dunbar Historic District, a focus of urban renewal in Dayton in the 1990s. Dunbar was editor of the student paper at old Central High School and president of the literary society. Later he worked as an "indoor aviator"—an elevator operator—in the Callahan Building at Third Street and Main, downtown. He sold copies of Oak and Ivy to his passengers. He was born in Dayton in 1872, the son of former slaves. Joanne M. Braxton wrote that though he "himself was never enslaved, he was one of the last of a generation to have ongoing contact with those who had been." Public birth records for people born in slavery—and in the decades after slavery—are often non-existent; age, in many cases, is reckoned by consensus or reputed truth. Perhaps Mary Marshall-Thiebold was the last slave to die, at 101, in Connecticut in 1959; perhaps it was Pinky Mayo, who died at 113 in 1971.

Dunbar's parents had separated when he was a child and his father—who had fought in the Civil War in a Massachusetts regiment—took up residence at the Soldiers' Home, on the Veterans Administration campus. Dunbar's mother had done

washing for white families, including the Wrights, the famous
Dayton "air pioneer" family, and Dunbar became friends with
Orville Wright at high school; between 1892 and 1908 the Wright
brothers—Orville and Wilbur—had a number of bicycle shops on
West Third Street, on the near West Side. They were descended
from the Van Cleves, a family that had been among Dayton's
first settlers; the Wrights named one of their bicycle models the
Van Cleve. Dunbar was heralded as being of "pure Negro" stock
and, that way, different from other "Great Men of Color" (in J. A.
Rogers' phrase) such as Douglass or DuBois who were of "mixed"
heritage. In 2008 Dunbar was still best known for his dialect
poems, such as "When Malindy Sings" and "When Dey 'Listed
Colored Soldiers." He married Alice Ruth Moore of New Orleans,
who had gone to Cornell and written there on Wordsworth and
Milton, but he was "[o]ne of her several marriages." On Douglass,
he wrote, "'Twas for his race, not for himself he spoke." The
Pennsylvania track crosses North Paul Laurence Dunbar Street at
an angle of approximately seventy degrees; the tops of the tracks
are flush with the pavement's surface for a very long distance.
The street is a north-south running street and the railroad line
is parallel to Wolf Creek, which flows southwest from its source
near Brookville, until it joins the Great Miami by Riverview Park
downtown. The crossing on North Paul Laurence Dunbar Street
was protected, in 2008, by a pair of flashing lights that dates from
the 1940s or the 1950s; the bridge over the creek lies just beyond
the crossing.

Black people had come to Dayton—and the counties around Dayton—in numbers by the 1830s. The nexus of black Dayton in the 19th century was east of the Miami River; the West Side was undeveloped, though by the end of the new century's first decade the near West Side was a "streetcar suburb." The Wright family lived on Hawthorn Street, which runs between West Fifth Street and Germantown Street, near the present-day offices of the Dayton Urban League and in proximity to several churches; the house has been moved to Henry Ford's Dearborn Village Museum in Michigan. In the 19th and early 20th centuries, black people lived south of the railroad station and stockyards, in what was a service industry area in 2008. Eastern Europeans peopled the West Side in the first decades of the 20th century and in the late 1940s and early 1950s—in my father's memory of his early days in Dayton—a remnant population remained; there were two Hungarian restaurants on the near West Side then, and a beauty salon. A Hungarian doctor had maintained his office on South Broadway, as the neighborhood "changed," and treated a black clientele until sometime after the Korean War had ended, my father remembered. His—my father's—own first office had been on Perry Street, in the 1940s, a half mile south of Dayton Union Terminal.

Dayton was named for Jonathan Dayton, a New Jersey politician, who had been involved in the Aaron Burr affair; arrested for treason in 1807 he was never tried. He had supported the Miami Canal project—which connected the townsite with the Ohio River at Cincinnati—"without hesitation" and he had been prominent enough among the land speculators of 1795 for the transaction of that year to also go forward under his name: the Dayton Purchase was a large swath of land in what are now Montgomery and Greene Counties—it lay between the Great Miami and Little Miami Rivers. Settlers—whites—arrived in 1796; prior to that Shawnee and Miami people lived in the area. The Treaty of Greenville, signed also in 1795, allowed or encouraged white expansion along both Miami rivers. Ohio became a state in 1803. A white, Daniel C. Cooper, surveyed and cut the Mad River Road between Dayton and Cincinnati and brought the first black woman of record into the area, in 1802; her name is not known but her children—Harry Cooper and Polly Cooper—were indentured servants to Daniel Cooper until they were adults. The town, Dayton, was established at the confluence of the Mad River, the Stillwater River, and Wolf Creek, all of which join the Great Miami River in what is now downtown. The difference between rivers and creeks or runs is ambiguous and local instances contradict even very general rules; the same is true of mountains and hills. The first railroad—the Mad River and Lake Erie Railroad—came to Dayton in January 1851; the first traffic on the line was between Dayton and Springfield, now the Norfolk Southern's route along the Mad River. The Cincinnati, Hamilton, and Dayton also completed construction that year and began regular service in September; this route is now followed by the CSX along the Great Miami River south of Dayton. In April 1853 the Dayton and Michigan Railroad Company began operating trains between Dayton and

Toledo, 150 miles away at Lake Erie, on the Michigan state line; the Cincinnati, Dayton, and Hamilton obtained the line via a lease "in perpetuity" in 1863 and it's now also part of the Chessie System, the CSX—it follows the Great Miami River north (going through the afore-mentioned towns of Tipp City, Troy, and Piqua) and continues past the river's headwaters at Indian Lake in Logan County. I had supposed Logan County to have been named for Chief Logan, who had been involved in Lord Dunmore's War in which Tecumseh's father died, but it was named for Benjamin Logan, who "fought Indians north of the Ohio River under the command of George Rogers Clark." The Dayton Flood of 1913 killed three-hundred people and resulted in construction of a series of dams—called, collectively, the Miami Conservancy District— during the following six years. (All the dams are north of Dayton, except for Germantown Dam to the southwest, near Germantown, on Twin Creek. Englewood Dam with its mile-long causeway is largest and closest to Dayton; it controls the Stillwater River's flow into the Great Miami. Nearby Taylorsville Dam, at Vandalia, is on the Miami River itself; Lockington Dam, north of Piqua, is on Loramie Creek, and Huffman Dam, a popular picnic site for Daytonians, is on the Mad River near Wright-Patterson Air Force Base.) The Dayton and Western Railroad began operating trains between Dayton and Indianapolis in October of 1853. This became part of the Pennsylvania Railroad's line from New York to St. Louis; this is the route that follows Wolf Creek, that in 2008 still crossed the West Side of Dayton.

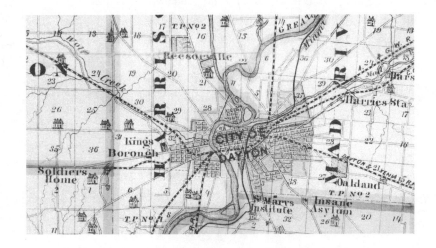

The Cincinnati and Springfield Railway Company came later, incorporating in 1870 and completing its line between Cincinnati and Dayton on January 1, 1871. This became the "Big Four Route" (the Cleveland, Cincinnati, Chicago, and St. Louis Railway), then the New York Central, and is now part of the Norfolk Southern. The line, in southern Montgomery County, is on the east side of the Great Miami River until it reaches the Dayton Power and Light plant at the southernmost edge of the city—the river bends there and the Norfolk Southern crosses it and enters the West Side on a long girder bridge; the CSX, in Montgomery County south of Dayton, is on the river's west bank. These two are the tracks that join at the grade crossing on

Washington Street on the West Side. In 1910, on the day following the hundred and thirty-fourth anniversary of the founding of the United States, the New York Times, under the headline "19 Dead in Wreck of Big Four Flier," reported that there had been an accident involving both railroads; a sub-head read, "Was Running on C., H. & D. Tracks and Crashed Into Freight Near Middletown, Ohio—Many Injured." Middletown is so named because it lies halfway between Dayton and Cincinnati; it "adjoins" the Great Miami River. The lines are parallel to one another and the Big Four train had been re-routed to the Cincinnati, Hamilton, and Dayton track because of a freight derailment ahead on its own line; a pilot engineer from the latter railroad was aboard to guide the train over his company's territory. The railroads are within earshot of each other as they come north, toward Dayton, along the river, from Cincinnati. Much in the article is unclear or incomplete—the direction of travel of the two trains is left to the readers' deduction and the central question of which train was to have overtaken the other, which seemed clear in the early part of the story, becomes an open question as the story progresses. Apparently one train was to have moved onto a siding while the other passed but they met in a head-on collision instead. A photograph existed, in 2008, on the Internet, reproduced from a glass plate in the George Grantham Bain Collection, showing the locomotives atop one another. "The crash when the two trains met was terrific," said the Times; and, "The engines locked into a mass of smashed steel and iron, the heavy passenger locomotive telescoping its smaller fellow as far as the cab." A lengthy and detailed list of casualties—deaths and injuries and residences—

appeared in the article which included, among the hurt, "Oscar Cubanissy, colored, Cincinnati, head and side injured," apparently the only non-white person injured or killed in the mishap.

In the "Colored People" section of Augustus Waldo Drury's History of Dayton and Montgomery County, the author notes, "The first negro in Dayton was in the community in 1798 and in the listing of taxpayers is included in the description 'William Maxwell (including his negro).' The colored girl that lived at Cooper's was therefore not the first but the second colored person at Dayton." Daniel Cooper came west, from New Jersey, at twenty "to look after the land interests of Jonathan Dayton" (who never set foot in Dayton); his Mad River Road, as noted above, was "laid out" in 1797 and provided the first overland connection between "the Mad River Country," as Dayton and environs was known, and Cincinnati. The "Cooper's" to which Augustus Drury refers is, in all likelihood, what came to be called Patterson Farm, a thousand acre parcel of land along the Great Miami River a mile south of downtown Dayton; Robert Patterson had purchased the land from Cooper in 1803. It stretched from what is now the University of Dayton to the site of the present-day Veterans Administration campus on the West Side. Patterson had come to Dayton from Kentucky accompanied by his slaves, Edward (or Ned) and Lucy Page; because the Ohio constitution prohibited slavery he called them "indentured servants" but they successfully contested the issue in court and, despite the efforts of a slavecatcher, David Sharp, apparently employed by Patterson to forcibly return the Pages to legal slavery in Kentucky, they managed to leave Dayton "for an unknown location."

Augustus Drury was a Jesuit; the University of Dayton was founded by and, in 2008, still headed by the Society of Mary. The Society of Mary also operated the boys' Catholic high school, Chaminade, on Ludlow Street in downtown Dayton, just south of the Dayton Union Terminal. In the 1950s and 1960s the school was understood to be "liberal" in social orientation and many middle class black families, few of whom were Catholic, sent their children there in an effort to thwart the "de-facto" segregation of the Dayton public schools. In the 1960s the Spirit of St. Louis was still running but it was, by that time, a "mixed train," passenger cars and freight cars combined in a single "consist." Another Pennsylvania Railroad train, the Penn Texas, also operated through Dayton in the 1950s and 1960s; it was possible, on this train, to book sleeping accommodations from New York to El Paso, Dallas, or Houston. The derelict, or residential, Lee and Alton hotels were located on Ludlow Street, between the train station and Chaminade High School; both hostelries—which served a white clientele—were in the shadow of the elevated railroad tracks. In later years the Patterson Farm was known as Rubicon, Robert Patterson having called it that in homage to Julius Caesar's crossing of the Rubicon River in 49 AD, during the Roman Civil War. The Patterson Homestead, built in 1810, is an example of Federal Architecture and in 2008 was operated by the City of Dayton as a museum.

By 1900 the black population of Dayton was 3500.

4.

MY FATHER, after graduating from Meharry Medical College, had interned at the Homer G. Phillips Hospital in St. Louis, where my mother was a school-teacher. Phillips, who had been a lawyer, died in 1931, victim of an unsolved murder. He had stayed with Paul Laurence Dunbar in Washington while he—Phillips—was in law school at Howard University. During that time Dunbar was working as a clerk at the Library of Congress but blamed the dust in the Library for his worsening tuberculosis and, after some travels, returned to Dayton alone in 1904 and died in his mother's house, on North Summit Street, in 1906.

When my father had finished his internship at Homer G. Phillips he returned to his native Birmingham to enter into practice with an older man whose name he could not recall in 2008, an arrangement set up by his own father, who was also a physician. When it became obvious that the partnership was ill-advised my father left Birmingham, intending to locate in Toledo, Ohio, where friends from medical school were already working. At the end of the second day of driving he had reached Dayton and drove through the city until he found the black neighborhood. There he located a café and met a pharmacist, another patron at the café, who encouraged him to stay for a few days and consider Dayton. After a week my father had decided to remain in the area. He and my mother were married at her parents' house on Cote Brilliante in St. Louis and, after a wedding trip to Buffalo, New York, came to Dayton. In 1949 they purchased the farmhouse at 161 Liscum Drive, two blocks south of the intersection with West Third Street, at the western edge of the city; this is the house in which my mother died in 2008. The farm's lands had been sold off as building lots but the house still sat on three quarters of an acre. Liscum Drive was racially mixed and in 2008 a few whites still lived on it. Liscum Drive did not continue north beyond Third Street so it was simply Liscum Drive, not South Liscum Drive.

Liscum Drive formed the western boundary of the Veterans Administration campus. From Liscum Drive a wide field, enclosed by a chain-link fence, led to the twin brick hospital buildings at the middle of the government property. Once, in the 1950s, someone landed a small airplane in the field and the curious "poured" out of the hospital to see plane and pilot; we had not imagined that the hospital buildings could contain that many people. The V.A. was on high ground, as previously noted; after the flood of 1913 people described its position as being atop a "natural levee." In 2008 the campus was still called locally by its old name, the Soldiers' Home. A system for caring for disabled soldiers had been established by the Lincoln administration in the days following the Civil War; the three initial asylums or homes that would provide this care were located in Togus (near Augusta, Maine's small state capital), Milwaukee, and Dayton. Black history in Dayton is intertwined with the history of the military—the Dayton facility was the first to admit black people, men who were veterans of the U. S. Colored Troops; as mentioned above, Joshua Dunbar—father of the poet—left his family to reside there instead.

Prominent on the V.A. campus is the Dayton National Cemetery; in it are buried veterans of the Revolutionary War, the War of 1812, the Civil War, the Spanish-American War, and all the 20th century wars and the wars current in 2008. Barring incident, burials will continue there through 2018. Some burials were accompanied by rifle-fire in the 1950s and 1960s; gun salutes are a practice dating back to the invention of firearms. Also during that time—the 1950s and 1960s—large striped tents were erected for mourners to stand beneath during burials and, because of this, interments "caught the eye" of passersby in automobiles or those riding trolley buses on West Third Street. In 2008 the cemetery had crept both east and west; it is near the fence that faces South Gettysburg Street and has extended up the small hill alongside Liscum Drive. The layout of the cemetery is acknowledged to be the work of Captain William B. Earnshaw, who is well known as a designer of military cemeteries. He, along with labor provided by the Colored Troops, disinterred and reburied the remains of thousands of dead soldiers.

Another time—in 1960 or 1961—convicts from the Workhouse, the Dayton Correctional Institute below Germantown Street, had been brought to Liscum Drive in a bus to work at maintaining the V.A.'s fence. One man walked away from the gang and, when the police arrived, we watched from the porch. The constable came—a rail-thin white man with grey hair wearing a plaid shirt, he stalked the fence with a large pistol in his hand, his fingers outside the trigger guard; the Dayton Police and the Jefferson Township Police also came—at the time, the early 1960s, the City of Dayton ended and Jefferson Township began just past the house in which we lived and there were questions of jurisdiction, of which police department held sway in a particular block.

In the cemetery well-paved roads named for states divide the graves—all of which are three-foot simple markers, made of the same white stone—into swaths. Interments and markers are provided without charge to veterans and their spouses.

West Third Street was and is the northern boundary of the V.A. and the grounds extend south from there to and beyond the Route 35 Expressway. The eastern boundary is South Gettysburg Street and in the 1950s and 1960s, on that street's first block below the intersection with Third Street, a row of taverns faced the V.A., each advertising a check cashing service. Veterans—who lived in the residence halls of the V.A.—would sign their monthly checks to the bartender and drink there until their stipends were exhausted. North of Third Street Gettysburg Street stretches all the way to Salem Avenue, the main street of the Dayton View neighborhood; North Gettysburg crosses Wolf Creek, at which point the Westwood neighborhood ends and Dayton View begins. Jews lived in Dayton View in the 1950s and 1960s as did Catholics. The Dayton View Catholics were white; their children went to the parochial high schools and referred to the neighborhood high school, Fairview, as "Fair-Jew." Fairview was an old high school; at the beginning of the 20th century students whose families lived west of the river had walked across the fields to attend it. In the 1950s and 1960s black Catholics lived in Edgemont, at the southeast tip of the West Side, where the Great Miami River's bending formed a bulb of land known by that name. Edgemont was the West Side neighborhood at the end of the Norfolk Southern (née Big Four Route) bridge across the river. In 2008 Dayton View was largely black, it had become a West Side neighborhood. All the West Side neighborhoods vary from one another but all are black. A few hundred feet south of the Wolf Creek bridge on North Gettysburg was another of the Pennsylvania Railroad's busy grade crossings, this one protected by automatic flashing lights and gates that would descend to block the path of approaching highway traffic. Until the mid-1960s the railroad track sat on a narrow embankment and the road, North Gettysburg Street, rose abruptly to cross it. Drivers proceeding north would stop first at the Western Avenue intersection and then climb sharply to the single track and ease their cars and trucks across it before dropping, as sharply, down the embankment's other side. The distance to the tracks was short, once the ascent began, but the ascent was slow and crossing the track itself was a tortured event. Because the automatic gates blocked only the approaching traffic's lane it was possible to drive around them when they were lowered. People misjudged the speed of approaching trains and the capabilities of their automobiles and this earned the crossing the nickname of "Old Bloody Gettysburg," a reference to the Civil War battle.

Deer and cattle and horses had grazed in pastures and groves that made up the bulk of the campus of the Soldiers' Home into the 1950s. In summer thunderstorms, blowing in from the west, would sweep across the field between Liscum Drive and the hospital buildings.

In 2008 North Gettysburg was a street of vacant lots, funeral homes, and small grocery stores. The most prominent funeral establishments were the House of Wheat and the McLin Funeral Home. Its founder, C. Josef McLin, Sr., had come to Dayton from South Carolina; he was charismatic and very good at business but was denied political power beyond the West Side. Later his son had a twenty-year career in the Ohio General Assembly and died in office in 1988. In 2008 the family business, the McLin Funeral Home, was located on North Gettysburg, near its intersection with Free Pike, a few blocks north of the House of Wheat. On North Gettysburg Street are also dealers in building materials—stone, lumber—and garden centers. Other funeral homes—H. H. Roberts, the Thomas funeral home, Townsend-Jones Brothers—are clustered around Gettysburg Street's intersection with West Third Street. In the vacant lots on North Gettysburg enterprising men have set up barbecue stands and sell ribs and chicken to passing drivers.

The crossing of the old Pennsylvania track was re-graded in the 1960s and Western Avenue, now named James H. McGee Boulevard, was moved three hundred feet south; the approach to the single track has been made gradual and North Gettysburg Street is divided by a cement island as it crosses the railroad. The crossing is

protected still by flashing lights—stationed at the right hand margins
of the roadway—and long automatic gates that descend to block all
traffic lanes; another pair of flashing lights—one set facing north, the
other facing south—is located on the cement island. It is a beautiful
railroad crossing—broadly situated, graceful, well-marked; if one
is looking north the woods that surround Wolf Creek are visible
beyond the tall striped gates. Wolf Creek Pike is the continuation of
James H. McGee Boulevard; west of Gettsyburg it swings northwest,
following creek and railroad, and crosses the track at International
Molasses, the last customer on the line. The railroad extends a mile
past that but that section is not used; in 2008 few trains crossed
North Gettysburg Street. In 2008 Google Maps showed the railroad
still following Wolf Creek far beyond Dayton. James H. McGee,
for whom Western Avenue was renamed, was Dayton's first black
mayor. He had been an undergraduate at Wilberforce and earned a
law degree at Ohio State University in Columbus. In 2008 C. Josef
McLin's granddaughter, Rhine McLin, was mayor of Dayton; she
had earned a Master's degree in guidance counseling from Xavier
University in Cincinnati and an Associate's degree in mortuary
science from the Cincinnati College of Mortuary Science. The track
across North Gettysburg Street had been the Panhandle Route, the
route of the Spirit of St. Louis and, later, the National Limited to
Kansas City, and the Penn Texas.

The old Pennsylvania line was the most formidable of
the tracks on the West Side; that is, it covered the most ground,
it traveled through the greatest number of neighborhoods, and its

gate towers—gone since the 1980s—were anachronistic heralds. The towers were gaudy; the gatemen accomplished their jobs in public, in the common sight of the neighborhood. The labor that was required to effect safety was a conspicuous labor.

The orientation of the West Side is east-west; that is, it is narrower and longer than it is "tall" in terms of the typical projection in which north is up. The axis of the West Side is West Third Street, along which the various black neighborhoods of Dayton accrete, and the West Side ends, five miles west of Third Street's river crossing, where the Crown Point neighborhood—the last black neighborhood, the westernmost extension of black Dayton—stops at Holland Avenue and becomes, with Elkins Avenue, the white Appalachian neighborhood Drexel which sits just past the Dayton city line. No natural or industrial boundary exists between the two—that is, no railroad or river divides white Drexel and black Crown Point and people from both places buy food at the Drexel Market, which they call by its old name, Stump's. Beyond Drexel, West Third Street becomes Eaton Pike, a well-maintained two lane road that carries U.S. 35 the twenty miles to Eaton, county seat of profoundly white Preble County, without curving. Beyond Eaton U.S. 35 joins Interstate 70 and crosses into Indiana as part of the national system of limited access highways; the highway bypasses downtown Richmond, which had been the first stop on the Spirit of St. Louis, Penn Texas, and National Limited trains west of Dayton. Travelers arriving in Dayton from the west or departing from Dayton on westward trips were allowed extensive views of the West Side as the train moved slowly across the neighborhoods both north and south of West Third Street. On the West Side the track made two wide curves as it passed through the length of black Dayton between Gettysburg and the Miami River, crossing all streets at grade and diagonally.

As a child I would sit in the Wilkes & Worth Barbershop on West Fifth Street and gaze at the trains crossing Mound Street—the track was two blocks south of the shop's plate glass windows—while the barbers and my father argued about national politics and about the contradictions of Negro life in Dayton.

Later, when I worked as an engineer, I would hate crossings like the one on Mound Street, the ones that came right on top of each other, following one another as points on a curve; I would approach with horn blaring but didn't care for the fact that the motorists couldn't see the train coming because of the curve of the track and structures, trees, etc., that would all block the line of their sight, no matter that the red highway lights were flashing.

Mound Street was in the part of Dayton named, first, Mexico and then Miami City. The street was named for the burial mound, "since gone," at its corner with West Fifth Street. The region—southwest Ohio—is indicated as lying between the "Pays des Miamis" to the west and "Pays des Eries" to the east on Jacques Nicolas Bellin's 1755 map, "Partie Occidentale de la Nouvelle France ou du Canada"; it was published forty years prior to the Dayton Purchase. In 2008, the area around Mound Street was "gentrifying" and passersby would receive the shock of seeing young white people standing in yards on the West Side.

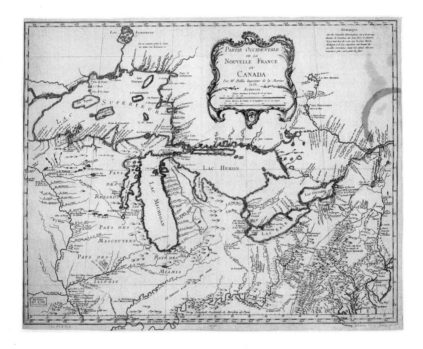

When the Pennsylvania track exited the West Side at Gettysburg it entered Madison Township and, a few miles later, the village of Trotwood. The village was named by its first postmaster or first stationmaster, who had been a devotee of Charles Dickens' work, for Betsy Trotwood, the character in David Copperfield. The railroad station in Trotwood was boarded up and in bad repair in the 1950s and

1960s but in 2008 it was well-maintained and recently painted; it had become a community welcome center. In 2008 the Pennsylvania line to St. Louis stopped a mile short of Trotwood but a blue Conrail caboose sat on a segment of track outside the station; the track was only slightly longer than the caboose. Cabooses disappeared from U.S. and Canadian railroads in the early 1990s and were replaced by computer transmission boxes mounted on the coupler of a freight train's last car; the boxes relay information about the status of the train—notably the brake pipe pressure—to the engineer and conductor, both of whom ride in the locomotive. The transmission apparatuses are called FREDs, for flashing rear-end device. It is the conductor, not the engineer, who is in charge of the train and in previous years the conductor would occupy the caboose; in the case of an emergency he was able to stop the train from the caboose by "dumping the air," which would apply all the brakes. In the 1950s and 1960s Trotwood and Madison Township were white areas—the latter was rural, the former was a sleepy town. In 2008 Trotwood was a black or largely black suburb of Dayton; geographically, the West Side expanded along its own natural boundaries—Wolf Creek and the railroad—through the 1970s and 1980s. The street named for the black mayor, however, stops at the Dayton city limit or, more correctly, it changes there into Wolf Creek Pike; it bears the name of a white family—the Wolfs were 19th century immigrants—that is also the name of an animal.

During the year that my mother was dying I dreamed of walking from West Third Street up a hill, at the top of which was a railroad crossing protected by crossbucks which had caught the light of the sun. A crossbucks, or crossbuck sign, consists of two white arms that form an X—on the arm that extends from the lower left to the upper right is printed the word CROSSING and on the other arm is the word RAILROAD, which is broken into two words—RAIL and ROAD—by its intersection with the unbroken word, CROSSING. Waking, I realized that the dream was, in essence, a memory of a scene I noted many winter mornings on my way to high school on the city bus. The bus route, Route One (Drexel westbound, Third Street eastbound), ran from one end of Third Street to the other end. Between its intersections with Gettysburg Street and Abby Street it paralleled the Baltimore & Ohio's line to the Veterans Administration campus; the track was on a ridge slightly above Third Street and a quarter mile to its south and it skirted the grounds of a housing project. On those mornings the sun, low to the horizon, would illuminate the metal arms of the crossbuck signs, visible from my usual seat on the Third Street bus. This had been a thing of visual moment.

The housing project was called Arlington Court. Its buildings lay along McCall Street—which was also parallel to West Third—between the Inland Steel complex, which began at Abby Street, and South Gettysburg; they were two-storey structures, boxy and pale colored. The project's gone now and the site has been leveled into a blank space. McCall Street ran from South Gettysburg east to intersect with Germantown Street at a 45 degree angle. Near its intersection with Germantown were the buildings of McCall Corporation, which had been the printing plant for many national magazines (*Life*, *McCalls*, etc.) until the 1960s. Arlington Court, my father remembered in 2008, was rough. "They shot each other on the weekends," he said. Between McCall Street and Arlington Court was the railroad; that is, the tracks were laid in a shallow depression that ran along the north side of McCall Street. Railroad crossings like the one I'd recalled with such clarity on waking from the dream described above were on South Hatfield Street and South Adler Street—the streets rose from West Third to the ridge where they would cross the railroad and then, a few feet later, meet McCall Street. The track existed, until the 1960s, so that coal could be delivered to the steam plant at the Veterans Administration—the line (clearly indicated on the 1875 map of Dayton, above) ended there. Now a truck brings the coal. Rail delivery was accomplished one carload at a time, effected by a single slow-moving switch engine; delivery necessitated the train stopping short of the South Gettysburg Street crossing and a crew member—the conductor—walking over South Gettysburg to unlock the gate into the V.A. before the train could proceed. I saw the operation just twice in all the years I lived in Dayton—a white man in coveralls with a ring of keys at the gate, the dark blue locomotive and its coal hopper at the other side of Gettysburg Street, at the lip of the pavement.

A train is defined by the Northeast Operating Rules Advisory Committee (NORAC) as being "[an] engine with or without cars."

5.

Home?

        That I saw
my mother's
      death there   as rain

                falling
                    on a RR bridge—

I was stalled   ridiculous
in a car
      between the tracks

& when I asked my father
                  what to do next
        he only said

        put the 4-ways on
so they'll see you
& know you're not a fool

      (the bridge
at that point over

I think
                    3rd Street
        but it snakes
                    all across downtown
to the east end of childhood Dayton

                                    the extent of which blurs
                or has become so, exaggerated,

    but with high cement sides,

                                all my life
                                    in whose shadow

    I have lived in California since 2007. I live in Berkeley, in a house on Grant Street built in 1908, forty-two years before I was born. Forty-two years prior to my mother's death in 2008 I was a sophomore at Chaminade High School in Dayton. I bought two paisley ties that year—one silk and one wool—and still occasionally wear the wool tie; ties were required for Chaminade students and I have maintained the habit—when I appear nowadays before my own students at the University of California I am dressed, more or less, as I dressed in parochial school.

    There is only one railroad line in Berkeley, the Martinez Subdivision of the Union Pacific Railroad; Berkeley's streets and neighborhoods climb gradually from San Francisco Bay and the tracks trace a water-level route—they are at the base of the hill, a mile from Grant Street, and follow the curve of the Bay. From Grant Street I can hear the trains blow for the grade crossings at Addison Street, Bancroft Way, and Hearst Avenue. There is an Amtrak halt at the foot of University Avenue; the Berkeley station-house has been converted into a restaurant, a common practice, and railroad passengers must purchase tickets at an automatic kiosk at trackside. The Capitol Corridor trains, which connect Sacramento with San Jose, stop at Berkeley; the San Joaquins, which run between Oakland and Bakersfield, do not stop at the Berkeley station and neither does the Coast Starlight, the overnight train from Los Angeles to Seattle.

A block east of Grant Street is Martin Luther King, Jr. Way. MLK, as it is called, parallels Grant Street and is a busy thoroughfare. Until 1984 the street was named Grove Street and, by "social custom," black people only lived west of Grove Street, on the downhill side. Black history in the East Bay—as Berkeley and Oakland are known— is connected to railroad history. Berkeley and Oakland are, in many ways, the same town; the major north-south streets—San Pablo, MLK, Shattuck, Telegraph, College—continue from one municipality to the other. Border neighborhoods overlap. In 1869 Oakland became the terminus for the transcontinental railroad and by the 1930s a third of the East Bay's Negro labor force worked for the railroad or for the businesses—such as the Pullman Company—that were its partners. West Oakland, which sat adjacent to the rail yards, became a black neighborhood; by World War II, Richard Walker wrote, "black settlement [had] extended into southwest Berkeley, which became a prestige address." The Grant Street neighborhood, through the latter years of the twentieth century, was "well kept" and "mixed"; in 2008 the neighborhood was largely white but several black churches continued to hold services on streets near to Grant Street—on clear Sunday mornings one could hear song emanating from a variety of locations.

Summers in Berkeley are cool and breezy; the warm weather arrives in September or October. In the winter it rains but thunderstorms are rare occurrences.

6.

In 2008 my parents owned two automobiles and when I went
out to look at the railroad bridge on East Third Street on the day
following my mother's death I took what she had considered to be
her car, the 1984 Toyota Camry. The car was basic and comfortable
and ran well. She had become ill the previous fall and declined
through the following three seasons, dying at the height of summer.
The following day I came to the bridge at mid-afternoon and drove
through its downtown neighborhood finding that to be a warren of
trucking companies and well-kept warehouses. A farmers market, the
Second Street Market, had taken over a building I recalled as having
been a railroad freight house in the 1960s; it had been open the day
previous, Saturday, the day of my mother's death, but it was closed
on Sundays. I discovered that there was a gravel road that led from a
trucking company's storage lot to the railroad itself and I drove the
Camry to within a few feet of the tracks. I wondered if I had in fact
found this access road earlier, during my high school years perhaps,
and forgotten it until I "saw" it again in the dream that I had years
later and, some years after that, transformed into the poem reprinted
in the previous section of this writing; on the Sunday following my
mother's death I realized that it would be possible for me to drive the
car onto the railroad tracks as I had done in the dream. It was a dry
realization—my mother had taught me to despise stupidity as though
it were an artless poison; in the dream my father had told me to pull

on the hazard lights in order to not be, or not appear to be, "a fool."
But the warning about being a fool was something more typical of my
mother's voice and wide outlook on the failures of life than my father's;
perhaps, in the dream's economy, he had undertaken her job or point
of view or language because she was dead and unable to communicate
the foolishness of my actions directly to me in her own voice. On the
day after she did die, I felt no temptation to force the Camry onto the
tracks. One can author destruction. But I did pull the hazard lights on,
both out of habit and because I had done that in the dream—I was
certainly in no danger of being hit by either rail or road traffic—and
stepped then out of the car and took a picture of the scene with my
cell-phone's camera; the tracks and ballast are a grey and brown blur
across the bottom of the photograph and the blue sky and its white
clouds, the bulk of the photograph, are nearly one texture.

Midwestern summers are hot; August is usually the warmest
month and Dayton temperatures during that time often reach the 90s.
The rainiest months are June and July but thunderstorms are common
between April and September and tornados occasionally come through
Ohio as well. The Xenia tornado of April 1974 destroyed half the
structures in that town and killed thirty-two people; the effects of the
storm are still evident in Xenia three decades later. The March 1913
flood, however, is still generally considered to be the most calamitous
weather event to have occurred in the Miami Valley—the flood, which
was caused by days of rain falling on snow, affected several rivers in
different parts of Ohio but was most devastating to Dayton. Rain in
Ohio generally originates in low-pressure systems in the southern

and western parts of the U.S. and, in both winter and summer, one can expect some precipitation every few days; thunderstorms, which usually include lightning, are more common in southern Ohio. The sound of thunder rarely travels for more than ten miles but the accompanying flash of lightning may be seen at a greater distance; such a "silent" flash is the familiar evening phenomena, heat lightning. A collection of "Safety Tips" issued by Lebanon, Ohio warns that, even though the storm that has produced the heat lightning may be far away, "the storm may be moving in your direction"; and the warnings continue—"Remember, lightning may strike some miles from the parent cloud. Precautions should be taken even though the thunderstorm is not directly overhead."

7.

Tecumseh meant "shooting star." He was venerated by the British
for his help in the unsuccessful War of 1812 and was praised by both
admirers and enemies for his good looks and eloquence; his idea
had been that a pan-Indian alliance against the depredations of the
whites was necessary and he had declined, for that reason, to offer his
signature at the Treaty of Greenville. Tecumseh's brother underwent
a religious conversion experience in 1805 and following that became
Tenskwatawa or "The Open Door"; he is more commonly known, in
historical discussions, as the Prophet. The brothers, following the loss
of Ohio, established a settlement to the west, called Prophetstown,
near the confluence of the Tippecanoe and Wabash Rivers. Tecumseh,
by rejecting the 1809 Treaty of Fort Wayne, which ceded much of
present-day Indiana to white settlement, earned the enmity of William
Henry Harrison, then governor of the Indiana Territory. Tecumseh was
not present at the Battle of Tippecanoe; the Prophet had assured his
followers that they were invulnerable to the bullets that would be fired,
at them, by white soldiers and when this turned out not to be true,
many deserted the cause of Tecumseh's confederation. On the evening
of Tecumseh's birth a meteor had fallen to earth and his father, seeing
it, named the baby for the celestial event. In the twenty-first century
one almost never sees an Indian in Dayton or anywhere in southwest
Ohio. Old Piqua, where Tecumseh was born, is variously described as
having been "near Springfield" or "near Xenia." "Shooting Star" is an

approximate, if roguish, translation; Albert Gatschet wrote that the name, Tecumseh (or Tekámthi or Tkámthi), "is derived from *nílani tkamináthka*, 'I cross the path or way' (of an animate being)," and that "Tecumseh and his brothers belonged to the *manetúwi msí-pessí* or 'miraculous panther' totem." Gatschet, a philologist, complained that "panther-lying-in-wait," "crouching lion," and "shooting-star" were all paraphrases of the *meaning* of Tecumseh "but do not accurately translate or interpret the name." He offered that "[the] adjective *manetúwi*, when it qualifies the noun *msí-pessí* as an epithet, points to a miraculous, unaccountable, even transcendental existence, and the whole must be rendered by 'celestial lion,' which is a meteor or shooting-star."

In Bible scholarship there is some debate about whether or not "Son of the Morning Star" refers to Satan. Isaiah said, "How art thou fallen from heaven, O Lucifer, son of the morning!" But this was apparently a reference to an oppressive king of Babylon; some readings of Luke suggest that Jesus was borrowing Isaiah's language when he—Jesus—remarked, "I beheld Satan as lightning fall from heaven." Elsewhere, in a commonly quoted passage in the Book of Revelation, Jesus claimed for himself the description "bright and morning star." Dr. Ronald H. Love, in the 14th Lesson of his "Christological Titles," says, "Its basis as a title for the Messiah was grounded in the prophecy of Balaam, 'I see him, but not now; I behold him, but not near—a star shall come forth out of Jacob, and a scepter shall rise out of Israel; it shall crush the borderlands of Moab, and the territory of all the Sherhites.'" Venus, the second planet from the sun, is the brightest star of the morning and this coincidence has been, over the years, widely remarked upon. The first dictionary entry for Lucifer, qualified as "Poetic," defines the word as "the planet Venus when it is the morning star"; the second is Satan and the third is "an early type of match ignited by friction." The noun—Lucifer—is from the Latin, light-bringing or light-bearing. Dr. Love's Christological Titles series does not shy from other symbologies: "George Armstrong Custer was dubbed by the Cheyenne in his military campaign to subjugate them as 'Creeping Panther,' for his ability to pounce unexpectedly upon an unsuspecting encampment. During the Dakota Campaign the Indians changed his name to the 'Son of the Morning Star,' for like Venus, he appeared out of nowhere and was seemingly everywhere. 'Morning Star' has established itself over time as an ever present god." An event's status changes over time; or a coincidence of events confers status. Elizabeth Hatmaker wrote, "Inevitably, the location cannot escape being named by (and for) the subject (even the marginalized one) any more than the subject can escape being named by the location." Venus, by virtue of its size and brightness and because of its appearance— at dawn and dusk—near the horizon, is the natural object most commonly mistaken for a UFO.

8.

When I drove my mother's Camry to the railroad on the day following her death I stopped before driving onto the bridge itself; there would have been ample space between the tracks and the cement side of the bridge but to drive there would have been to invite the notice of the Dayton Police. I did walk onto the bridge though and I stood and looked west for a long time, over its parapet, out Third Street before returning to the car and quitting the scene. Beyond the buildings of downtown the West Side was visible but, owing to the typical humidity, it appeared as a haze, a merger of shapes, a merely distant location. A train came while I loitered on the bridge, a mixed freight—containers, boxcars, tank-cars, etc.—led by two CSX locomotives. It was headed for Toledo or Detroit, having come up from Cincinnati on the old C., H. & D. main along the Miami, having crossed the river and come across the long bridge through downtown. I felt its presence in the air before I heard it, though the difference is rather fine.

When does railroad sense begin? Perhaps it's sourceless, or a particular kind of sourcelessness. Perhaps it is a degree of inevitability in which location is a prime factor, though certainly not the only factor. There's a relationship between the railroad and its stations—the union stations, such as the one in Dayton, as well as the small depots in towns connected by the tracks. Or railroad sense begins with a train in the street like an elephant wandering there: a little dirty, a little sweet smelling, the tang of slowness. Trains shuttle, elephants bob and shuffle. Locomotives are often coupled together "elephant-style": that is, when a train is heavy enough to require two or more locomotives to lead it the locomotives will often be set up so that both, or all, are facing front. On September 24th, 2008 I watched the northbound Coast Starlight cross Fruitvale Avenue in Oakland and made a note of it in the journal I'd been keeping then. I remarked that the train was going fast and that the two GE engines were "coupled elephant-style," the phrase coming to me instantly.

END

CITED

"19 Dead in Wreck of Big Four Flier," *New York Times*, 5 July 1910.

Dallas Bogan, "History of the Little Miami Railroad," 2004, The USGenWeb Project. www.rootsweb.ancestry.com/~ohwarren/Bogan/bogan414.htm

"Dayton Union Ry. of Dayton-Ohio," Annual Summary Report of operations of all railroads operated by the New York Central Railroad System, 1952.

Joanne M. Braxton, "Paul Laurence Dunbar," in *The Concise Oxford Companion to African American Literature*, edited by William L. Andrews, Frances Smith Foster, and Trudier Harris (New York: Oxford U. Press, 2001).

Carolyn J. Burns, "History of Dayton, Montgomery County, Ohio." http://www.carolynjburns.com/history.html

Priscilla Cardenas, International Society of Sons and Daughters of Slave Ancestry. http://resources.rootsweb.ancestry.com/~guestbook/cgi-bin/public_guestbook.cgi?gb=898&action=view

"Jonathan Dayton," Wikipedia. http://en.wikipedia.org/wiki/Jonathan_Dayton

A. W. Drury, *History of the City of Dayton and Montgomery County, Ohio, Volume 1* (Chicago: S. J. Clarke Publishing Co., 1909).

"Alice Ruth Moore Dunbar-Nelson," LSU Libraries, Subject Guides: Louisiana Leaders: Notable Women in History. http://www.lib.lsu.edu/sp/subjects/lawomen

"Paul Laurence Dunbar," The Library of Congress, American Memory. http://lcweb2.loc.gov/ammem/today/jun27.html

"Paul Laurence Dunbar (Jun 27, 1872 - Feb 09, 1906)." http://www.dunbarsite.org/biopld.asp

Paul Laurence Dunbar, *The Life and Works of Paul Laurence Dunbar: Containing His Complete Poetical Works, His Best Short Stories, Numerous Anecdotes and a Complete Biography of the Famous Poet* (New York: Dodd, Mead, 1907).

L. H. Everts, *New Historical Atlas of Montgomery County, Ohio, Illustrated* (Philadelphia: Hunter Press, 1875).

A. S. Gatschet, "Tecumseh's Name," *The American Anthropologist*, Vol. 8, Number 5 (1895). http://www.jstor.org/stable/658447?seq=2

"Elizabeth Burgess Harvey Mendenhall / September 22nd, 1801~May 1st, 1888 / and her husband / Dr. Jesse Harvey / November 26th, 1801 ~ May 12th, 1848." http://www.docstoc.com/docs/89760952/ ELIZABETH-BURGESS-HARVEY-MENDENHALL

Elizabeth Hatmaker, "City Confidential: On the Lyric Mapping of Urban Space," *Language and Learning Across the Disciplines*. http://wac.colostate.edu/llad/v6n2/hatmaker.pdf

Herbert Hill, *Black Labor and the American Legal System: Race, Work, and the Law* (Madison: University of Wisconsin Press, 1985).

"Lightning Safety," City of Lebanon, Ohio. https://www.lebanonohio.gov/index.aspx?NID=206

"Little Miami Railroad," Ohio History Central. http://www.ohiohistorycentral.org/entry.php?rec=744

"Benjamin Logan," 2005, Music Entertainment Network. http://www.music.us/education/B/Benjamin-Logan.htm

"Logan," Ohio History Central. http://www.ohiohistorycentral.org/entry.php?rec=243

Dr. Ronald H. Love, "Christological Titles." http://www.centralmethodist.net/e-study/Christological%20 Titles/14%20-%20Bright%20Morning%20Star.pdf

"Luke 10:18," Bible Hub. http://biblehub.com/luke/10-18.htm

"Mayor Rhine McLin," Institute for Supply Management. http://www.ism-mv.com/speakers/Mayor%20 Rhine%20McLin.pdf

"Middletown, Ohio," Wikipedia. http://en.wikipedia.org/wiki/Middletown,_Ohio

"Train wreck near Middletown, Ohio." Shorpy Historical Photo Archive :: New York-Cincinnati Flyer : 1910. http://www.shorpy.com/node/270?size=_original

Northeast Operating Rules Advisory Committee, *NORAC Operating Rules* (Philadelphia Conrail Operating Manuals, 2000).

"Page, Lucy and Edward (Ned)," University of Kentucky Libraries, Notable Kentucky African-Americans. http://www.uky.edu/Libraries/NKAA/subject.php?sub_id=45

"Partie Occidentale de la Nouvelle France ou Canada," The Library of Congress. http://www.loc.gov/ item/73695755/

"Robert Patterson (pioneer)," Wikipedia. http://en.wikipedia.org/wiki/Colonel_Robert_Patterson

Leonard Peacefull, *A Geography of Ohio* (Kent: Kent State U.P., 1996).

"The *Penn Texas*," Streamliner Schedules. http://www.streamlinerschedules.com/concourse/track3/penntexas194812.html

"Map of the Pennsylvania Railroad," Map Directory. http://mappery.com/maps/Pennsylvania-Railroad-System-Map.jpg

Poor's Manual of the Railroads of the United States (Cleveland, Lorain and Wheeling Railway, 1901), Newberry Library Cartographic Catalog: map catalog and bibliography of the history of cartography. http://www.biblioserver.com/newberry/index.php?m=word&kid=17722795&gid=1&iid=

Tom Pulsifer, 7 April 2004, Railroad Forums, "Xenia." http://www.railroad.net/forums/viewtopic.php?f=129&t=1184

"The National Soldiers' Home and Cemetery in Dayton—Reading One," National Park Service. http://www.nps.gov/history/nR/twhp/wwwlps/lessons/115dayton/115facts1.htm

John Speller, US Railroads, "The Cincinnati, Hamilton & Dayton Railroad." http://spellerweb.net/rhindex/USRH/CHDRR.html

"Tecumseh," Ohio History Central. http://www.ohiohistorycentral.org/w/Tecumseh?rec=373

"Tecumseh falls short of dream of tribal unification, Indian purity," Pittsburgh Post-Gazette, Local News. http://old.post-gazette.com/localnews/20030817lewisbar0817p8.asp

Philip Valenti, The Schiller Institute, "Paul Laurence Dunbar / The Struggle for an American Classical Renaissance." http://www.schillerinstitute.org/educ/dunbar.html

"What Dreams We Have," National Park Service. http://www.nps.gov/history/history/online_books/daav/chap1.htm

"About Wilberforce University," Wilberforce University. http://www.wilberforce.edu/welcome/index.html

"Wright-Dunbar Village," National Park Service. http://www.nps.gov/daav/historyculture/wrightdunbarvillage.htm

Writers' Program of the Work Projects Administration, *The Ohio Guide* (New York: Oxford U.P., 1940).

C. S. Giscombe's most recent books are *Prairie Style* and *Into and Out of Dislocation.* He teaches poetry at the University of California at Berkeley where he is also curator of the Mixed Blood poetry and talks series.